# CHICHEN ITZA

Cover:
Temple of the Warriors: the Columns and
the Chac Mool
Photography: Vicente Santiago

Text: Susana Vogel

Photographs:
Vicente Santiago
Enrique Franco Torrijos
Walter Reuter
Irmgard Groth
Archives Monclem
 INAH ✿

Translated by: David Castledine

© 1995 by Monclem Ediciones, S.A. de C.V.
    Leibnitz 31, Col. Anzures 11590
    México, D.F., México.

Printed in Mexico
Impreso en México
ISBN 968-6434-24-0

# Index

# The Maya culture

*Figurine from the Island of Jaina showing both the typical Maya physical features and the adornments worn by members of the higher classes; the stylized headdress with a small fringe over the forehead and the facial scarification achieved by first applying color to the skin and then making a design using incisions.*

The Mayas created one of the great cultures of Mesoamerica during the pre-Hispanic era, building ceremonial centers where they developed mathematics, astronomy and the calendar, hieroglyphic writing, architecture and various aspects of art and culture. The Mayas occupied a wide area with such geographically diverse features as the mountains of Central America, the Peten region of Guatemala and the limestone plains of the Yucatan Peninsula. Their territory stretched over what are now the states of Campeche, Quintana Roo, Yucatan, Tabasco and eastern Chiapas in Mexico, most of Guatemala, Belize and the west of Honduras and El Salvador. As a result, their cultural traits were similar, but show local variations.

In ancient times the Mayas were divided into groups having similar physical characteristics, speaking languages that belonged to the same linguistic stock and sharing a common historical tradition. Research by experts has shown that around 2500 B.C. a group speaking Proto-Maya lived in what is now Huehuetenango, Guatemala. In time, this ancestral language split up into the different Mayance languages, and migration of the groups eventually led to the definition of the area where the Maya culture developed.

These migrations not only caused separation into different groups but also brought them into contact with the members of other cultures. This explains why experts have different opinions about the origins of the Maya culture. Some assert that it arose in the mountains of Guatemala, where they began to grow maize, and later moved to the north and west, without denying the possibility of influence from other cultures including Olmec as one of the most important. Others believe that it originated in northern Tabasco and southern Veracruz where the groups that would later form the Maya culture came into contact with the Olmecs in about the 10th century.

The Olmec culture is often called the "Mother Culture" since various ideas were taken from it that were used in the later development of other great cultures, and its influence stretched from its home on the Gulf Coast to different regions of Mesoamerica. The Mayas adopted and adapted several features of Olmec culture, including architectural elements and the basic number and calendar system that would later become the accurate Maya calendar.

Maya chronology is similar to that of the rest of Mesoamerica but is more precise because explorations of the area have produced complete sequences of pottery, and the deciphering of time hieroglyphs has made it possible to correlate it with our own calendar.

At the beginning (500 B.C. to 325 A.D.), although the typically Maya was beginning to appear, particularly in the clay figurines of humans that show their characteristic physical features, Olmec influence is still present, as can be seen in the decoration on some of their first buildings.

From 325 A.D. Maya culture began to develop and spread; external influences disappeared, the typical corbel arch was used in buildings and important dates referring to history and myths were recorded in hieroglyphs. Culture and art reached their peak between 625 and 800 in such areas as the calendar, astronomy, architecture, sculpture and pottery; numerous cities and ceremonial centers were founded.

All this splendor came to an end between 800 and 925 A.D. for reasons as yet undetermined, although possible ones are the exhaustion of agricultural land, changes in climate and a rebellion of the lower classes against their rulers. Maya culture slipped into decline; both cities and ceremonial centers were practically abandoned and in time covered by vegetation.

For the next 50 years only isolated groups remained in the area. Their cultural level was low since all those who understood the calendar and the keepers of various types of knowledge were gone. With them, Maya culture proper had disappeared: a period followed that shows other cultural influences.

From 976 to 1200 A.D. the Maya tradition became mixed with the Toltec originating from central Mexico, and the cult of Quetzalcoatl began —the Toltec god called Kukulcan on the Peninsula. Toltec influence is also evident in building and decoration as art began to imitate what there had been at Tula, but modified by Maya artists. At this same time, ties were created between the governing families of different cities, for example the one between the Xiu of Uxmal, the Itza of Chichen and the Cocom of Mayapan around 1000 A.D. Little by little Mayapan was gaining supremacy and between 1200 and 1540 there were conflicts between towns governed by families of Nahua origin and those ruled by Mayas. As a result, in about 1441 the Xiu of Uxmal attacked Mayapan and massacred the Cocom, which finally divided the population and impoverished their culture. Although the Mayas tried to reinstate their former tradition they only succeeded in bringing back the use of their language, and when the Spanish arrived on the Peninsula they found a people that had lost its luster.

The pre-Hispanic Mayas were one of the most amazing civilizations of their times, with clearly defined social strata. The elite devoted themselves to trade, war and religion. Architects, who belonged to the same rank, planned buildings while stonemasons were in a socially inferior class along with governors' servants and the different craftsmen.

Finally, the lowest class was composed of farmers, who grew mainly maize, beans and squash together with yucca, manioc and sweet potato.

Priests were very important as they directed ceremonies and rites to honor the gods and seek their favors. Among the most important deities where the creator, *Hunab Ku*, the god of Rain, *Chaac*; the lord of the Heavens, *Itzamna*; the god of Wind, *Ik*; the patron of Cacao and War, *Ek Chuak*; the goddess of the Moon and Childbirth, *Ixchel*; and the god of Death, *Ah Puch*.

Astronomers, who devoted their time to finding harmony in the universe and its recurring cycles of time, had to make complicated calculations to predict natural events and connect them with the fate of the population; scribes recorded history, religion and mythology using a complicated system of hieroglyphs, while painters and sculptors depicted both mythical and religious subjects as well as the deeds of governors. In architecture, characteristic elements were combined to produce the different styles of Peten, Palenque, Rio Bec, Chenes, Puuc and finally Maya-Toltec.

Their numerical system was vigesimal; symbols were given a value according to position and the concept of zero existed. Three symbols were used in writing numbers: a dot for one, a bar for five and a stylized shell for zero. All other numbers were written by combining these. The Mayas also devised glyphs for the numbers 0 through 19, which were often used instead of the other system.

Maya philosophy is very special, since no other culture of the period was so obsessed with time. Like other peoples of Mesoamerica they had two calendars; the ritual one, called *Tzolkin* that was used for calculating religious ceremonies and festivals and predicting the destinies of people, and the solar calendar or *Haab*, containing 18 months of 20 days each plus five unlucky days called *uayeb* ($18 \times 20 + 5 = 365$ days). The two calendars were used in conjunction, and the Maya calculations were so accurate that they were able to make exact reckonings, predict eclipses and plot the orbit of the planet Venus.

*This glyph from the Temple XV at Palenque, Chiapas, is part of an inscription referring to the life and work of the leader* Chan Bahlum. *It shows the Sun God, one of the main deities of this city.*

## CHRONOLOGICAL TABLE

| PERIOD | | DATES | CHARACTERISTICS |
|---|---|---|---|
| FORMATIVE OR PRECLASSIC | | 500 B.C. to 325 A.D. | Influences from other groups, particularly the Olmecs, were evident, but the Maya element began to assert itself, especially in the clay figurines that show typical ethnic features. |
| C L A S S I C | EARLY CLASSIC | 324 - 625 A.D. | External influences disappeared and typical traits begin to show, such as the Maya vault in buildings and the recording of important dates with hieroglyphs. |
| | FLOWERING | 625 - 925 A.D. | Art and culture were at their peak in architecture, sculpture, mathematics, astronomy and hieroglyphic writing. |
| | DECLINE | 800 - 925 A.D. | Maya culture went into decline: cities and ceremonial centers were abandoned. |
| TRANSITIONAL OR INTERREGNUM | | 925 - 975 A.D. | Culture descended almost to the level of the Formative period. |
| MAYA-TOLTEC OR MEXICA | | 975 - 1200 A.D. | Invaders arrived, bringing with them influences from Nahua-speaking groups and the Toltec culture of central Mexico. The cult of Quetzalcoatl —in Maya Kukulcan— arose. Alliances were made between cities governed by Mayas and others ruled by families of Nahua origin. |
| MEXICA ABSORPTION | | 1200 - 1540 A.D. | Conflicts began; alliances were broken; wars divided the people and culture became impoverished. |

# Chichen Itza in History

*The Castillo at Chichen Itza in a lithograph by Frederick Catherwood (1844)*

The name of the city may mean "Mouth of the Itzas' Well", from *chi*, mouth; *chen*, well, and *Itza*, the name of the Maya group that settled there. However, other Mayanists interpret it as meaning "At the Edge of the Well of the Water Sorcerers". In the north of the Yucatan Peninsula there are no surface watercourses and rainfall is scant, so "cenotes" (*dzonot* in Maya), which are natural cavities formed when the limestone surface collapses and leaves underground water exposed, were essential to the population. Therefore, the cult of Chaac, god of Rain and Waters, was very important and involved various ceremonies and propitiatory rites.

The cenote of Xtoloc in Chichen Viejo ("Old" Chichen) provided the city with water, while the Sacred Cenote was dedicated exclusively to the worship of Chaac. Here priests and diviners performed sacrifices and made their predictions, and all this is related to the fact that the Itza were thought of as "Water Sorcerers".

The history of Chichen Itza probably begins when the Itza arrived and settled there. One theory says that they were Chontal-speaking Mayas established in Champoton and anciently related to Nahua-speaking groups; that their trading activities led them to sail around the Yucatan Peninsula, when they landed first on the island of Cozumel, from where they later made their way to Chichen. Another possibility that other researchers claim is that the Itza came from the Peten region of Guatemala, through Bacalar, Quintana Roo, and years later migrated to Chichen and settled there.

An exact chronology based on studies made by the great Maya expert Dr. Sylvanus Morley indicates that the Itza reached Bacalar between 415 and 435 B.C. and then went on to Chichen between 456 and 405, settling there between 495 and 614. Later, between the years 514 and 692 they abandoned the site and migrated south, establishing themselves in Champoton between 692 and 731. They stayed here until 968, then returned to settle in Chichen in 968-987. Finally, at some time between 1194 and 1204 Chichen was conquered by the Cocom when the Mayapan Alliance or League broke up and led to the Itza being expelled from their territory.

Some researchers say that the Itza first subjugated the original inhabitants of the site and then held power for a long period of time. Their leader, believed to be descended from the gods, had the roles of priest, judge and chief of warriors and had several assistants who exercised power in his name in the places under their jurisdiction.

These members of the higher classes, as well as having the functions mentioned above were also guardians of knowledge about religion, mythology, astronomy, mathematics, medicine and the arts. Merchants were included in this class.

Merchants were extremely important since the economy was based largely on trade, which they carried out by exchanging products with the other groups that came to Chichen for religious celebrations and on market days. They brought various goods with them from their home regions and bartered these either for cacao beans or for different local products.

Over the years, many structures and temples were built at Chichen Itza that were linked by causeways called *sacbe* in Maya ("white road") for ease of communication. These include one running from the Castillo to the Sacred Cenote; one linking the Well of Xtoloc and the Observatory or Caracol; another that begins at the Ball Court and runs west, and one between the Nunnery and the Temple of the Three Lintels, as well as other less important ones.

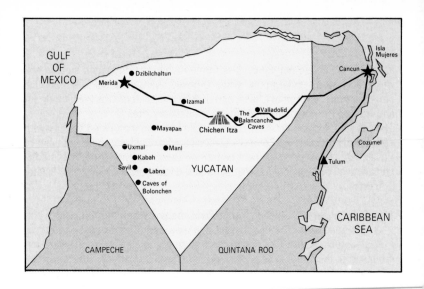

The Itza worshiped Kukulcan, whose cult was introduced by the Toltecs arriving from central Mexico. The importance that this god grew to have in the city is shown by the large number of representations of him either as a feathered serpent or as a man-bird-snake.

The cult of *Chaac* the god of Rain was also very important since it was related to the healthy growth of crops essential to the livelihood of the inhabitants. In fact, some researchers believe that he was the most highly venerated deity. He is portrayed many times on the different structures in the form of masks with the characteristic scrolled nose. Other gods were also worshiped such as *Ah Puch* or *Yum Kimi* the god of Death and the Underworld; *Itzamna*, lord of the Heavens, and *Ixchel*, goddess of the Moon and Childbirth.

Some of the earliest buildings are in the Puuc style, which flourished in the north of the Yucatan Peninsula, with decoration based on stone mosaics on friezes, latticework panels, columnettes, and embedded columns on the corners of buildings. Others are in the Chenes style, with decorated friezes and roof crests. Toltec influence began towards the end of the Classic period and so during the post-Classic Toltec style decorative elements were added, such as eagles and jaguars devouring human hearts, Chac Mool figures, "atlante" statues (telamons) and feathered serpents.

After the conquest of Yucatan in 1547 some chroniclers mention Chichen Itza, particularly Bishop Diego de Landa in his *Relacion de las Cosas de Yucatan* ("Account of the Things of Yucatan"). Many of the names given to the buildings on the site are in fact due to the interpretations made of them by the Spanish at the turn of the 16th. century. After this, Chichen lay forgotten and covered by jungle.

In the early 1840's John Lloyd Stephens, an American explorer turned diplomat investigated Chichen and other sites in the Maya area accompanied by the British draftsman Frederick Catherwood. The result of this was the publication of "Incidents of Travel in Yucatan" (1843), which revealed Chichen to the world.

Later, and as result of these accounts, other travelers and explorers reached the site to study the buildings. Among these were Desiré Charney, Alfred P. Maudslay, Agustin (Augustus) le Plongeon and Teobert Maler, who were there in the late 19th. century. In this century Edward H. Thompson, the American consul in Merida, bought the land where Chichen stands and explored the Sacred Cenote. He recovered many objects from the well, including beads, pottery, bones, jade and gold, most of which were sent to museums abroad.

Shortly afterward the site was taken over by the Mexican government and explorations were begun in the 20's with Mexican archaeologists working alongside researchers from the Carnegie Institution of Washington on the task of restoring the different monuments. Work was later continued by the Mexican government through the Institute of Anthropology. Chichen Itza is now considered one of the most important of the many archaeological sites in Mexico.

*At the spring and fall equinoxes crowds of visitors gather to watch the symbolic descent of Kukulcan to Earth down the north staircase of the Castillo. A fiesta is held at Chichen Itza during these days.*

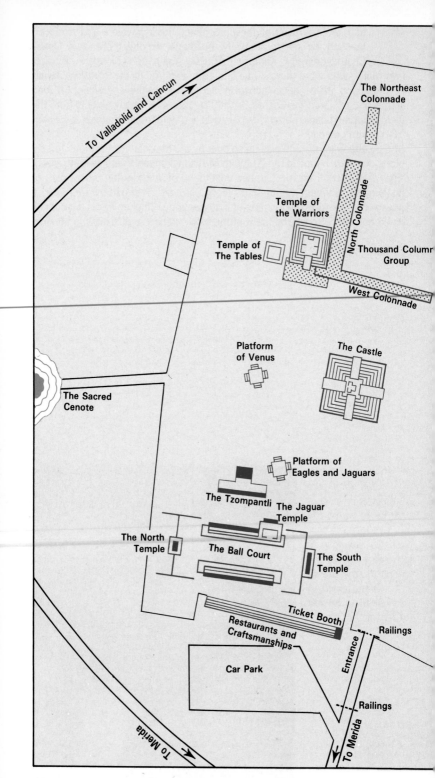

To Valladolid and Cancun

The Northeast Colonnade

Temple of the Warriors

Temple of The Tables

North Colonnade

Thousand Column Group

West Colonnade

Platform of Venus

The Castle

The Sacred Cenote

Platform of Eagles and Jaguars

The Tzompantli

The Jaguar Temple

The North Temple

The Ball Court

The South Temple

Ticket Booth

Restaurants and Craftsmanships

Railings

Car Park

Entrance

Railings

To Merida

To Merida

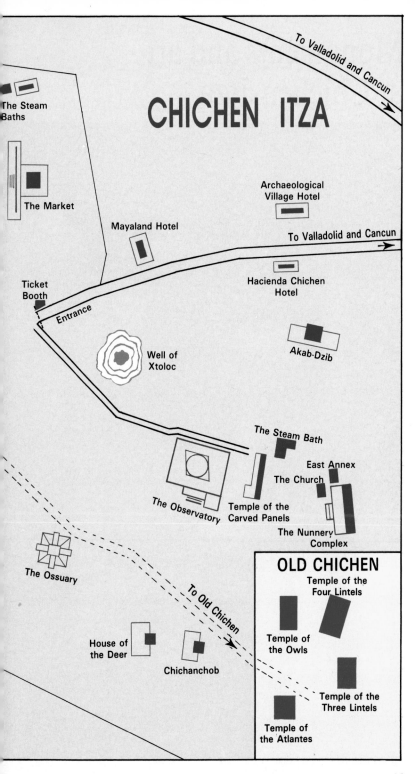

CHICHEN ITZA

The Steam Baths

The Market

Mayaland Hotel

Archaeological Village Hotel

To Valladolid and Cancun

To Valladolid and Cancun

Ticket Booth

Entrance

Hacienda Chichen Hotel

Well of Xtoloc

Akab-Dzib

The Steam Bath

The Observatory

Temple of the Carved Panels

East Annex

The Church

The Nunnery Complex

The Ossuary

To Old Chichen

House of the Deer

Chichanchob

OLD CHICHEN

Temple of the Four Lintels

Temple of the Owls

Temple of the Three Lintels

Temple of the Atlantes

# Monuments and art at Chichen Itza

**The Castle** or Pyramid of Kukulcan is a magnificent Toltec influenced structure 24 meters high with a square base, nine recessed stories symbolizing the planes of the underworld, and a small temple on the top. The use of sloping walls is striking, as is the decoration of raised rectangles. It has four great staircases of 91 steps, one on each side, and the north one finishes at the base in two colossal heads of feathered serpents.

The temple consists of a small vestibule with an entrance divided by two columns in the shape of serpents with gaping jaws; the bodies are the column shafts, their tails support the lintel and their heads form the bases.

The inner chamber has two pillars decorated in bas relief that supported the roof beams, a sloping face and a vertical wall with a frieze on the upper part between two cornices, and three stone tablets. Surrounding the other three sides of this chamber there is a narrow gallery with doorways onto the south, east and west staircases. On the main entrance to the temple there is a mask

of the god Chaac, the roof is topped by merlons shaped like cross sections of conch shell, symbols of the god of Wind and the jambs are carved with figures of priests and warriors.

Inside the Castle is a smaller pyramid containing another temple, a red throne in the shape of a jaguar and a Chac Mool sculpture. This inner structure is the result of the custom of building over temples, covering them with a larger one at the end of the 52 year cycle.

The great temple of today is related to astronomy: at 3pm on the spring and fall equinoxes (March 20 and September 21) the sun forms a series of seven isosceles triangles of light and shade on the ramp of the north staircase which gives the impression of an undulating serpent. The effect has been identified with the symbolical descent of the god Kukulcan to Earth to begin the agricultural cycle.

**Light and sound show.** Throughout the dry season, which lasts for eight months in this region, a show is held at night at the Castle that combines lighting with music and spoken accounts of Chichen Itza's history. The monument is spectacularly illuminated.

**The Castle staircase.** On each side of the Castle, which is one of the most imposing monuments on this site, a staircase leads up to the temple. At the foot of the ramps flanking the northern one there are huge, impressive heads of feathered serpents carved in stone. Their open jaws show their fangs, and their long tongues are carved with half-circles representing the movement of the Sun, probably related to the god Quetzalcoatl-Kukulcan.

The worship of poisonous snakes such as cobras and their use as symbols was common among ancient civilizations; Mesoamerican cultures featured the rattlesnake. This cult was introduced into the Yucatan Peninsula by Toltec invaders towards the end of the Classic period. They affirmed their power and imposed their religion, art and culture, as can be appreciated in architecture and decoration typical of their culture.

**The Red Jaguar in the Castle.** This throne or altar was found in the smallest of the pyramids contained in the Castle. In the shape of a jaguar, which was sacred to the Mayas, it is painted red and has incrustations of jade and bone. On its back there is a turquoise disk where offerings of copal resin could have been burned.

**The gold disk from the Sacred Cenote.** This disk of hammered gold was recovered from the Sacred Cenote at Chichen Itza. It shows a scene that may depict a fight between Toltec warriors from central Mexico and Mayas. It could also represent the defeat of the Itza, since it shows a Toltec chief accompanied by a spear-carrier threatening a Maya warrior, who offers him his reversed weapon as a sign of surrender; between them is a wounded Maya. The upper edge is engraved with a rattlesnake.

**The Sacred Cenote.** This is a natural well at the end of a 300 meter long causeway that runs north from the Great Plaza of the Castle. It was used only for religious, ceremonial and ritual purposes, as it was dedicated to the cult of Chaac, god of Rain and Water. The well is 60 meters in diameter, and its amost sheer walls fall 22 meters to the surface of the water, itself some 20 meters deep. The bottom is a thick layer of mud, and the water is different shades of green because of the algae and microorganisms present in it.

Parts of the walls are in their natural state, but several man-made alterations can be seen on the south side. The edge here was adapted to make tiers for the spectators watching the ceremonies and rites held there.

The well was considered a sacred site, where children, virgins and warriors were sacrified, thrown in from an irregular shaped platform on the edge. At one side of this platform there is a steam bath where victims were ritually purified before being sacrificed.

Several explorations of the bottom were carried out between 1882 and 1968 and valuable, archaeologically significant objects were recovered that originated from several different places. This proved that there were pilgrims who came from their homes either near Chichen Itza or from as far away as Central America to leave offerings to the god worshiped there.

Skulls of the human sacrifices and a large number of other objects were discovered: gold and copper bells; gold disks engraved with historical or religious scenes; pyrite disks and mirrors; jade beads; balls of copal resin and rubber; carvings of snake heads and rattles; wooden objects such as stools, handles and a staff of office; standard-holders in the shape of jaguars; copper rings and sandals; carved stones from the Ball Court; clay vessels and cooking pots, and arrow heads.

**Temple of the Warriors.** This magnificent structure, built over an earlier one, has a base measuring 40 meters along each side and 12 meters high. Its tiers with sloping walls are topped with a cornice carved with jaguars and eagles devouring human hearts.

The temple proper has two chambers and is reached by a staircase with carvings of feathered serpents running along its sides, with their heads at the top. Above these there are some warrior sculptures that served as standard bearers. A Chac Mool sculpture lies in front of the entrance to the temple between two columns in the shape of feathered serpents that form three openings into the first chamber of the temple.

The entrance has carved lintels and the pillars inside are carved with figures of Kukulcan, warriors and persons of rank. The second chamber contains pillars and an altar supported by "atlantes" (telamons) that is built into the rear wall; the exterior walls combine Maya and Toltec decorative features.

Above the cornice on the lower part there are masks of the god Chaac in the Puuc style and a high relief of the human face of Kukulcan between the jaws of a serpent. The staircase then leads to the upper platform with two vaulted chambers that contain the remains of murals belonging to the earlier structure known as the Substructure of the Warriors or the Temple of Chac Mool, since this is where a statue of this type was found.

## Mask of Kukulcan-Quetzalcoatl.

A prominent feature on the lower cornice of the sloping wall in the Temple of the Warriors is a mask of Kukulcan-Quetzacoatl. He appears with a human face, between the jaws of a serpent. The background of the mask is made up of bird claws and feathers carved in low relief, combining into the man-bird-serpent symbol. The decoration is completed with Chaac Mask in the Puuc style.

All this illustrates a combination of Maya and Toltec design motifs associated with the mythology and religion of the two cultures: Quetzalcoatl was the major god in Tula and Teotihuacan, and Kukulcan in Chichen.

**The "Atlante" Altar in the Temple of the Warriors.** The second chamber of this temple contains an altar set into the rear wall, supported by small "atlantes" (telamons). These typical Toltec features came to be included in the buildings of Chichen Itza between 1000 and 1250 A.D. and are warriors usually wearing the pectorals, belts and wrist-bands that were customary parts of their professional attire.

**Head of Staircase. Temple of the Warriors.** The ramps bordering the staircase up to the Temple of the Warriors end on both sides in large stone heads of feathered serpents with gaping jaws showing their fangs. These form the base of two sculptures of warriors each with their hands joined in front to make standard-bearers where the banners of the Itza and their governors could have been placed.

**Temple of the Warriors: the Columns and the Chac Mool.** In front of the entrance to this temple there is a wide platform with a stone statue of Chac Mool. This Toltec style offertory figure in its typical half-reclining position with its head turned to one side and a vessel held between its hands has been interpreted by some researchers as the messenger between man and the gods.

It is positioned between two large, splendidly carved feathered serpent columns that symbolize the god Kukulcan. The tails of these serpents originally supported the lintels of the entrance while their heads, in this case decorated with horns, form the base of the pillar.

**The Steam Bath.** This has an entrance hall with four columns and stone benches set into the walls. A small doorway leads into the steam room, and at the far end of this is the oven where rocks were heated before water was thrown over them to produce steam. A drainage canal carried away the water, and some small openings high up in the walls allowed smoke to escape and provided ventilation.

**The Market.** There is no proof that this structure was in fact used as a market. It stands on a low platform with steps at the two ends and in the center. The main room is a gallery with high walls at the rear and columns and pillars at the front and sides. A stone bench is set into the walls and next to the entrance there is an altar decorated with human figures at the bottom and feathered serpents on the cornice. The entrance used to be decorated by pilasters carved with various persons of high rank. Behind the gallery, the pillars surrounded a square patio and may have supported a roof made of wooden beams and palm leaves.

**Thousand Columns Group.** A large number of columns and pillars, many of them beautifully carved, surround a spacious square patio. The columns and their capitals held the joists supporting the rubblework vaults. The columns stand in distinct areas and are therefore known as the North, Northeast, East, Southeast, West and Northwest Colonnades.

**Carving in the Thousand Columns Group.** The Thousand Columns Group is in the Maya-Toltec part of the site, and many of the columns and pillars in it are finely carved with different motifs. This is a high relief of a richly dressed dignitary wearing a large feather headdress, earplugs and nose plug, and illustrates the magnificence of governors' and priests' dress. The upper class also wore short cotton coats decorated with feathers, sandals, and jade, obsidian and shell jewelry. Jaguar skin was sometimes used in clothing.

27

**Platform of Eagles and Jaguars.** This square platform has a staircase on each side with large heads of feathered serpents at the top. On the walls there are panels carved with reliefs of eagles devouring human hearts, and others showing jaguars in the same attitude. The cornice shows reclining warriors.

**Decoration on the Platform of Eagles and Jaguars.** This belongs to the Maya-Toltec period and shows a marked influence from the Nahua culture of Central Mexico. Eagles devouring human hearts decorate the raised panels, while on the sunken ones jaguars with beautifully carved markings do the same. Both these animals are associated with the sun's journey across the sky during the day and its descent into the underworld at night. Also, they are both directly related to warriors, whose main duty was to take prisoners for sacrifice.

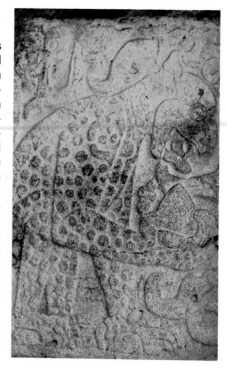

**Platform of Venus.** This is another square platform with a staircase on each side flanked by feathered serpents whose bodies run the whole length and end in large heads. The wall panels are decorated with allusions to the planet Venus, which was studied by Maya astronomers. Spanish chroniclers report that various ceremonies were held on these patforms.

**Decoration on the Platform of Venus.** The decoration combines several different elements: the sunken panels are carved with the sign of Venus between the open jaws of a serpent. On the raised panels the planet is symbolized by the sign for the month "pop", and a bundle of rods represents the years. The cornice shows a serpent surrounded by fish.

**The Tzompantli.** The name means "Wall of Skulls". It is a rectangular platform decorated with symbols of death, and was where the heads of sacrificial victims were displayed. A low sloping base supports a cornice, vertical wall and then another cornice all decorated with reliefs of skulls on stakes. The cornices end in snakes, eagles eating hearts, warriors and feathered serpents, all showing the influence of Central Mexico.

## Decoration on a Column at the Entrance to the Jaguar Temple Annex.

The pilasters at the entrance are carved with motifs similar to the ones decorating the walls and vault: figures of warriors in low relief and different depictions of the god Kukulcan, including one of him as a man-bird-serpent.

This column shows a dignitary wearing the clothing and with the insignia that correspond to his rank: a sort of eagle helmet, ear ornaments, pectoral, wristbands and a spear decorated with feathers.

**The Jaguar Temple and its Annex.** The platform on the east side of the Ball Court was shortened to build a base that is reached up a narrow staircase; from there another flight of steps up to the temple is flanked with reliefs referring to Kukulcan. The temple itself consists of an entrance gallery and one room containing an altar where there are remains of murals, including a battle scene involving the Itza.

The upper frieze shows two feathered serpents with entwined tails, and in the middle are the jaguars that gave the temple its name. These walk away from each other towards three shields, the symbol of war. On the lower frieze there are intertwined serpents.

At ground level behind the temple stands the small Annex with just one, beautifully decorated room. Two square columns separate the entrance into three bays, and in the center one stands a stone throne in the shape of a jaguar, an animal associated with the power of Maya governors.

**Entrance to the Jaguar Temple.** The entrance has three bays formed by two large columns carved as imposing serpents whose tails support the lintels and heads are the bases. Both the lintels and the jambs are decorated with warrior figures.

**The Ball Court.** The great Ball Court at Chichen Itza in the "I" shape typical of all Mesoamerica measures 168 by 70 meters, making it one of the largest in the Maya area. It is bounded in the east and west by platforms with vertical faces, and in the north and south by rectangular temples. Set high up halfway along the sides are the stone rings that were goals. The complex has staircases up to the top of the platforms, where there are structures that could have been benches for the spectators.

Benches with sloping faces run along the bottom of each side wall. These are decorated with panels carved in relief showing richly dressed players walking towards the symbol of death.

The game had important mythical and religious meaning, linked with deities that symbolized the eternal struggle between light and darkness, as well as with the movement of the heavenly bodies. However, it was also a form of entertainment that demonstrated the players' skill, since the rubber ball could only be propelled with knees or hips. In its more worldly form the game attracted heavy betting.

**Ball Court Goal.** A hit on one of the rings high up on the ball court walls scored but, as reported by Spanish chroniclers after the Conquest, because it was so extremely difficult to shoot the ball through the ring, when a player managed to do it his team automatically won the game. These goals were carved with designs connected with both the protector gods and the heavenly and mythological symbolism of the game.

This stone ring from the court at Chichen Itza is carved with entwined feathered serpents that represent Quetzalcoatl-Kukulcan, the principal god of the inhabitants.

**Relief on a Ball Court Bench.** The religious and ritual aspects of the game are well illustrated by the striking reliefs on the sloping faces of the benches lining the sides of the court. A magnificently dressed player wearing protection on his arms and right knee as well as the classic ball-players' padded belt kneels and is beheaded by a member of the opposing team. Blood spurts from his neck in the form of a serpent to then become garlands of flowers and leaves.

The sacrificed player bends towards a central, ballshaped motif where a skull with the symbol for words coming from its mouth represents death. A molding of a serpent with a head at each end stretches along the top of the scene. This illustrates the importance that the ball game had in Mesoamerica, since it is believed that the winner had the honor of offering his life to the gods by being beheaded. This practice, for which prisoners of war were also used, seems to have been common on the Gulf Coast and on the Yucatan Peninsula, and was connected with the fertility of the earth.

**The North Temple.** This building stands at the north end of the Ball Court. The temple has a single room profusely decorated with low reliefs that feature Kukulcan with warriors at his sides and thirteen other persons. On the rear wall there is the curious carving of a bearded face.

**South Temple**. This building adjoins the south side of the Ball Court. It has a single room and an undecorated facade, a cornice between moldings and a frieze, and six pillars in the entrance carved with warrior figures and above them the hieroglyphs for their names. The panels inside show Kukulcan between the wide open jaws of a feathered serpent.

**The Ossuary.** Also known as the Tomb of the High Priest, this building stands on a ruined base that used to have stairs decorated with entwined serpents, their heads at the top. It consists of a shrine surrounded by a gallery formed by the portico. Between its first two pillars there is the mouth of a deep cavity where seven graves were discovered containing various offerings such as shells, bells and figurines of rock crystal and jade. Stone steps set into the wall lead to a natural cave associated with the World of the Dead.

**House of the Deer.** It owes its name to the tradition that there used to be a deer painted on one of the inside walls. It is a small temple standing on a platform with rounded corners reached up a centrally placed staircase. The facade and the frieze are plain and separated by composite moldings. It has a large, plain roof crest that is in ruins.

**Chichanchob** or "Little Holes" owes its name to the pierced roof crest. Another name for it, "Red House", comes from the red band painted around the portico. This temple, standing on a base, has two galleries; one is an entrance hall and the other has three rooms with the typical Maya vault. The facade has a plain frieze, lintels and a double roof crest.

**Akab-Dzib.** This consists of two chambers and two buildings with eight galleries roofed with Maya vaults that join together in the north and south. The facade has a roof crest and frets; over the south entrance there is a stone lintel with the figure of a priest surrounded by hieroglyphs that have not yet been deciphered and which explain the name of "Obscure Writing".

**The Observatory.** This building is also known as the Caracol and belongs to the Transitional period between 900 and 1000 A.D. It consists of a rectangular platform in one tier with sloping walls plus a cornice with rounded corners. This measures 67 meters north-south, 52 meters east-west and is 6 meters high. A staircase on the west side is decorated on both its sides with entwined serpents.

A circular base was built on this platform 11 meters in diameter. and 3.70 meters high whose cornices have moldings and masks of the god. Chaac. This in turn supports another circular structure with a sloping base, protruding molding and a vertical wall topped with another molding.

In front of this base there is a terrace 20 meters by 6.5 meters with a vertical wall and molding that was later covered by another terrace surrounded with stone incense burners in the shape of human heads. On the terraces stands the round tower

that is the actual observation chamber. This building, which begins from the first base, shows that the original structure was formed of a simple nucleus already containing the spiral staircase ("escalera de caracol") from which the building takes its name.

The staircase led to the observation chamber then, when the other two bases were added, the core was enlarged with another room; later the terrace surrounding the tower was built. The spiral staircase leads to the observatory, which is a small room with narrow slits in the walls through which the movements of the stars were studied.

Maya astronomers succeeded in plotting the position of different bodies and made it their task to observe their movements. Using their extremely accurate astronomical and mathematical calculations as a basis they evolved a solar calendar, *Haab*, of 365 days divided into 18 months with 20 days each, plus five "empty" days and a ritual calendar, *Tzolkin*, that governed the life of peoples and the individual destinies of men. The two were used in conjunction with each other. It was also the astronomers' responsibility to try to find harmony in the constantly moving Universe and its recurring time cycles. Maya thought was of course distinguished by the constant preoccupation and reflection about time.

**The Observatory Tower.** This is a cylindrical building with one small chamber from which Maya astronomers studied the heavens through observation slits. They achieved their astonishing astronomy, such as recording the solar, lunar and Venusian cycles, calculating eclipses of the sun and the movements of constellations such as the Pleiades (which they called *Tzab*) using rudimentary instruments in special buildings like the Caracol. Astronomy was closely linked to their concept of the world, since the cosmos was regarded as the scenario for the sacred forces, and the heavenly bodies were gods on whom human life depended.

**The Nunnery Complex.** Because of its numerous small rooms and the belief that these were inhabited by priestesses dedicated to certain ceremonies it was given this name by the Spanish in the 16th century. The largest structure dating from the Classic period, it was built in several stages over the centuries. First the platform was laid, which was then enlarged and a frieze between two moldings added around the top, as well as a staircase to the new, higher level.

An extension was then built against the south, east and west sides with a frieze at the top between two moldings that is decorated with masks of the god Chaac and panels of latticework. Finally another addition was built over the structure with a narrower staircase leading up to the second story. This staircase is bordered by vertical stone rings and divided by a small building halfway up. The small temple on top has only one room.

The facade is decorated with columnettes between two cornices, and on the terrace there are two temples, each containing two galleries of six rooms. The north facade is decorated with latticework, small columns and squares, while the south has small columns and squares and carved rosettes.

**The Church.** The building was given this name because is stands close to the Nunnery Complex; it dates from the 7th and 8th centuries, when the Puuc style flourished. It has a single, rectangular room covered by a vault, with an entrance on the west side. The decoration is both profuse and symmetrical, based mainly on stone mosaic. The frieze on the facade has three masks of Chaac, the god of Rain, positioned at the center and on the corners. The masks which look like the stylized scrolled noses typical of depictions of this god, are the most striking decorative features.

These alternate with four other figures placed two by two in niches that have been interpreted as the four *hacab*, deities that hold up the sky. Here they take the shapes of an armadillo, conch, turtle and crab, each standing at one of the four cardinal points. Running along the top of the facade is a serpent figure, and three Chaac masks project from the top of the roof crest. In the lower part, the frieze is bordered by a molding of stepped frets —a decorative feature that can also be seen where the roof crest begins. On the sides and rear of the building there are several different motifs including frets, masks, and a toothed band on the cornice showing a simplicity in decoration that contrasts with the richness on the face of the building.

**The Nunnery Annex.** This is one of the most beautiful and harmonious buildings in the Chenes style at Chichen Itza. The rectangular construction contains three parallel galleries each with two rooms, plus two that were added later on the east and west sides. The north and south faces are decorated with panels of latticework and the two corners of the front are topped with masks of Chaac, the god of Rain. The frieze, which is framed by moldings, also contains masks. The two upper moldings run round the whole building and between them there is the carving of a writhing serpent.

The east face has a wide variety of decorative elements on it, including masks and figures with up-curved noses (symbol of the Rain God). Some of them are positioned around the top of the doorway, giving the impression that the entrance is through open jaws. This might be associated with the passage to the world of the gods.

Above the molding that bends up over the entrance there is a medallion framed by frets; in the center is a seated human figure wearing a feather headdress. The north and south faces have moldings topped with symbols of rattlesnake tails that seem to have been added to the building in a later period. The lintel of the doorway is carved with a hieroglyphic inscription that has been deciphered

as corresponding to 800 A.D. The top of the whole building is surrounded by a molding with cornice and it seems originally to have had a roof comb on the front, according to a drawing that Frederick Catherwood made when he visited Chichen in the middle of the last century.

## Medallion on the Nunnery Annex.

The high lords of the Maya ruling class wore elaborate headdresses as both adornment and symbol of their power. These were made from the plumes of various birds, including the tail feathers of the quetzal, which lives in the tropical forests of southern Chiapas and Guatemala. The importance of the seated figure above the entrance to this striking building is evidenced by his splendid headdress. The medallion is framed by frets and masks.

## Temple of the Carved Panels.

This stands on the east side of the Great Plaza and was built in two stages. First, the temple was erected on a base. It has an entrance with three bays formed by two serpent columns and a single room with a built-in bench. Later, another room was made with access through a doorway with four columns, containing a double row of columns and a bench running along three of its walls. The original staircase was demolished to make way for another that passes through the roof to reach the temple.

## Detail from the Carved Panels.

On the exterior side walls of the building finished in the second stage there are the beautifully carved panels that give the temple its name. They have three rows of low relief carvings that include several different motifs such as warriors, gods, birds, monkeys, jaguars, trees and a hut with three people.

## Temple of the Initial Series.

There is a complex of temples in Old Chichen called the "Date Group", and the most important of them is the Temple of the Initial Series. This is because it holds the only hieroglyphic date discovered so far in Old Chichen. It reads "10.2.9.1.9., 9 Muluc 7 Zac", plus another in the abbreviated system of "10.2.10.0.0, 2 Ahau, 13 Chen", and corresponds to 879 A.D. This Classic Maya data is carved on a lintel that was later rested on top of two monumental, Toltec-inspired "atlante" columns. Maya inscriptions usually begin with the "Long Count" or *Initial Series* which indicates the *baktun* (cycles of approximately 400 years), *katun* (20 *tun* (years), *uinal* (20 *kin*) and *kin* (days).

## Temple of the Atlantes.

This is a small building whose main decorative feature is a entrance framed by two large "atlante" figures. As part of their costume they are wearing pectorals, wristbands, belts and nose-plugs, all typical elements that make them identifiable as warriors, who wore all these items to identify their profession and rank. The positioning of their arms and hands seems to indicate that they originally supported the base of the roof. This type of sculpture is typical of the Toltec influence from central Mexico that gradually fused with the Maya culture,

## Temple of the Owls.

Standing in the vegetation of Old Chichen, the only remains of this temple are some pillars carved with these birds. These were probably associated with the night or else were seen as omens of death and disaster. The owl seems to have been introduced onto the Yucatan Peninsual as a decorative element by the Toltec invaders, because other birds appear fairly often in Maya iconography, shown either realistically or combined with human features to create fantastic, mythological creatures.

## Temple of the Three Lintels.

This stands on a rectangular base and has three chambers with doorways topped by carved lintels. One of these bears a date corresponding to 850 A.D. The upper part of the facade is decorated with a writhing serpent, bundles of four columns and Chaac masks at the four corners.. The rear is decorated with latticework panels and engaged columns.

## The Balancanche Caves.

These caves, whose name means Throne of the Sorcerer or of the Jaguar, are five kilometers from Chichen Itza. Passages stretch for some 800 meters inside, following a stream that ends in a small lake. In the cavern walls there are some niches where sculptures were found. In the middle of the main chamber stalagmites and stalagtites join to form a pillar where vessels, urns and figurines were discovered together with a large number of incense burners and miniature *metates* (saddle querns) that had been placed there as offerings to Chaac.

## Caves of Yucatan.

There are many caves in the state, for example Loltun, near Oxhutzcab. These are tunnels with extraordinary rock formations that give the sections their names. Figurines and ancient petroglyphs have been discovered here as well as a sculpture dating from the Classic period that depicts the lord of the hills. The caves of Bolonchen (*bolon* = mine, and *chen* = well) near the village of the same name are very deep. At the bottom of them there is a pool (*cenote*) with streams branching off to run underground to other wells. This was visited by Frederick Catherwood, who drew the impressive ladder leading to the bottom.

Printed in
Repeticiones Gráficas, S.A. de C.V.
Pacífico 312, Col. Rosedal, Coyoacán
04330 - México, D.F.
4000 copies, April, 1998